Fortress

Old town-main gate

IE OLD HARBOUR

Dubrovnik
Maritime
Museum

St. John´s
Fortress

ADRIATIC SEA

E

S

25 50 75 100 m

Dubrovnik

Dubr

AUTHOR: © Fernando Espinosa Chauvin, COPYRIGHT, 2010 **TEXTS:** Branka Milisic, Bill Halby **SPECIAL THANKS:** Dijana Gugic and tour guide Ivan Vukovic **ART DIRECTION:** Romulo Moya Peralta **PRODUCTION MANAGER:** Juan Moya Peralta / TRAMA **ARTS:** Amelia Molina Segovia, Meliza de Naranjo / TRAMA **FIRST EDITION,** january 2010 **DESIGN AND PRODUCTION:** TRAMA PUBLISHERS **PRE-PRESS:** TRAMA **PRINTED IN CROATIA:** Graficki Zavod Hrvatske d.o.o. **TRAMA:** Juan de Dios Martínez and Portugal N34-367 Quito, Ecuador **PHONE:** (593 2) 2 246 315 / 2 255 024 **EMAIL:** editor@ trama.ec http://www.trama.ec / www.libroecuador.com **ISBN:** 978-9978-369-15-9

Fernando Espinosa Chauvin

ovnik

tramaediciones

Text: Branka Milisic

Dubrovnik
the pearl of the Adriatic

Once called "the pearl of the Adriatic" by poet Lord Byron, Dubrovnik is an exotic walled city lying on the coast of the sparkling Adriatic Sea at the tip of an isthmus in southern Croatia, part of what was once the Republic of Yugoslavia. With its mild winters and hot dry summers, colorful history astounding architecture, Dubrovnik with its red-tiled roofs is a sun-drenched magnet for tourists that pour into town through its own international airport several cruise lines and a network of local bus transportation. The settlement was founded on a rocky island named Laus (nowadays the South part of the city), which provided them shelter from Slavic and Avars attacks. The name Laus -- in Latin "the rock" -- gradually changed to Lausium -- Rausium -- Ragusium -- Ragusa and until the 15th century was used to refer to the city. Later on, the Slavic people grew their settlement at the foot of the forested Srd Hill. The name Srd is actually the Slavic version of the Latin ***Sergije*** -- the guardian that symbolically denotes that the hill was a true "guardian" of Dubrovnik. This settlement, and in particular the oak woods that in the past surrounded the city, give to the city its Slavic name "Dubrovnik" which means oak forests mostly found in abundance in the hills north of the city. (dub-oak, dubrava-forest)

The area around Dubrovnik was first inhabited several thousand years before Christ (by some estimates 6000 years, and 2000 to 3000 by others). The origins of the city were lost through the cloudy course of history. Legends are interwoven with historical facts, but there are no preserved documents from those ancient times or so few that historians and archaeologists are left to speculate about the ancient life around Dubrovnik. One thing is certain: Dubrovnik is an old city standing on its stone cliffs for at least 14 centuries. Before Dubrovnik, there was a much older Roman city, ***Epidaurum*** which developed in the area where Cavtat now lies, 18 kilometers southeast of Dubrovnik. Until the time of its demise in the 7th century, ***Epidaurum*** existed for at least 10 and perhaps as many as 12 centuries. Some historians have stated that the Greeks founded the colony as early as the 7th century before Christ. ***Epidaurum*** spread along the coast, with its great, beautiful and famous structures. It was second in size on the Adriatic coast only to Salona (which according to some historians was surpassed in size only by Rome). There are claims that ***Epidaurum*** may have had up to 40,000 residents. For a time, this city was at an important crossroads for the Roman Dalmatian province.

A great earthquake in the middle of the 4th century destroyed ***Epidaurum*** and a part of the city sunk into the sea, where it still lies buried under thick layers of sediment. However, the city continued to exist. Too weak to fend off the attacks by many nations (the Celts, Goths and Vandals), at the end of the 5th century it fell into the hands of the eastern Goths and was liberated in the middle of the 6th century with the help of Byzantium, which later took on the role of ruler and protector. Later the city was unable to defend itself from the forceful attack by Avars and their allied Slavic tribes. It was finally conquered and destroyed in about the year of 614, when it experienced complete ruin.

However, recent findings have brought up some doubts regarding the origins of Dubrovnik. The renovation of the cathedral revealed that beneath its structure there are remains of the church dating from the 5th century. In addition to that, there have been discoveries of city wall segments also dating from the 5th century. This could confirm the thesis of some historians that settlements on this territory date back long before the 7th century.

Due to its advantageous location Dubrovnik was known throughout history as a maritime trading port, rivaling even that of Venice. Although a small city-state, Dubrovnik developed a naval power with one of the best fleets of merchant ships in the Mediterranean, with a reputation for excellence in the building of wooden galleons and large ocean-going vessels called carracks. Carracks were big, stable ocean going ships which were quite roomy in order to carry provisions for long voyages. Carracks were made of wood, with three masts measuring up to 10 meters in length and up to 30 meters in width. According to some sources, carracks could transport 1500 to 2000 barrels of different goods. They were used to import grain from southern Italy and Sicily and to export wood and salt. The Argosy fleet, as it was called, consisted of over 200 ships that transported goods of foreign merchants to far-flung ports, from India to America, as documented in the ships logs which included names of famous captains and descriptions of ports visited. Also the oldest contract of maritime insurance in Dubrovnik dates back to 1395 and the Maritime Insurance Law of Dubrovnik ***"Ordo super assecuratoribus, 1568"*** is the oldest in the world.

By the laws of the Dubrovnik Republic, every ship had to have its scribe, who recorded the names of captains, ports visited, ownership contracts, and other information. One day of sailing by carracks would cover approximately 52 nautical miles, or the distance from Dubrovnik to Budva (Montenegro) or from Dubrovnik to Lumbarda (at the island of Korcula). The fame of the Dubrovnik carrack is even recorded by Shakespeare in his play "The Merchant of Venice."

Originally under the protection of the Byzantine Empire and throughout its history, surrounded on all sides by foreign powers, Dubrovnik managed through skillful diplomacy, international trade, and sheer determination to successfully balance its claim to sovereignty against the interests of Venice, the Ottoman Empire, and other foreign enemies. Negotiating favorable merchant terms for themselves, Dubrovnikians often turned enemies into friends. During the 17th century when the Venetians took advantage of the European offensive on the Turks to completely cut off Dubrovnik from the Ottoman Empire, the Dubrovnik Republic was able to avoid Venetian enclosure and keep its hinterland by creating a corridor between what are now Bosnia and Croatia through the sale of two parcels of territory to the Ottoman Empire which prevented a borderline with Venice.

Between the 14th and the 19th century Dubrovnik governed itself as a free city-state. In 1806 the city fell to Napoleon and the French. After the Congress of Vienna in 1815 the Habsburg Empire took over from the French. Foreign domination continued until the fall of Austria-Hungary in 1918, when Dubrovnik was incorporated into the new Kingdom of Serbs, Slovenes, and Croats, which later became the Kingdom of Yugoslavia. During World War II Dubrovnik was occupied by the Germans and Italians. Following a civil war, Dubrovnik became part of Communist Yugoslavia under Tito and, in 1991 part of the breakaway Independent Republic of Croatia. Dubrovnik once again fell under siege, this time from the Serbs. In May of 1992 Dubrovnik was liberated by the Croatian army. Though under the continued threat of attack during the next three years, the damage caused by Serbian shelling of the Old Town was largely repaired by 2005.

Throughout its long history, there were many foreign rulers who visited Dubrovnik, including Richard the Lion-Hearted who during a storm became shipwrecked there in a Venetian ship on his return from the Third Crusade. As the storm raged, the king vowed to build two churches to the Blessed Virgin Mary if he survived, one on the first spot where he would step on land and the other in his homeland. He found shelter in a small cove on the island of Lokrum and keeping his promise intended to build a church there, however a delegation of twelve aristocrats persuaded him, with the Pope's approval, to build a cathedral instead in Dubrovnik. The construction of the cathedral began in the 12th century and was finally completed in the 14th century. The existing Baroque cathedral was constructed on the foundations of the original Romanesque structure, which was destroyed by the catastrophic earthquake of 1667. The rich cathedral's reliquary contains the relics of saints, which are brought out once a year during the time of the St. Blaise ceremonial procession.

The disastrous earthquake of 1667 was one of the crucial milestones for Dubrovnik. The earthquake was followed by fire and the city suffered great damage. Around 1,200 people were killed. The entire city was destroyed except the City Walls, Sponza Palace, Rector's Palace and some churches and a few private buildings. The fact that the Sponza Palace survived the earthquake probably saved the Republic of Dubrovnik; it continued to perform state affairs in spite of the heavy damage to the city. It took thirty long years after the earthquake to reconstruct the city, the citizens showing fierce determination to restore Dubrovnik's prosperity. However, the earthquake was not the only cause of Dubrovnik Republic's subsequent decline.With the discovery of America and the emergence of other European naval powers, merchant routes moved to the Atlantic Ocean and Dubrovnik no longer held a monopoly in trading.

The name "Sponza" derives from the word "spongia-alluvium" that denotes the spot where rainwater was collected. Throughout history, the Palace had various functions – custom office, warehouse, mint, bank, treasury, and armory where today its first floor houses the Dubrovnik archive.

Dubrovnik began to develop its tourism in the 19th century. Intellectuals such as Lord Byron, George Bernard Shaw and Agatha Christie were stunned by Dubrovnik, which became a major tourist destination in post-war Yugoslavia. The opening of the first hotel – Miramare –in 1868 and the even more luxurious Hotel Imperial in 1898 marked the beginning of the expansion of modern tourism which became the most important economic branch of commerce in the next century. However, in the 1990s it was abruptly interrupted by civil war. The Imperial Hotel (now the Hilton) was completely destroyed by fire during fierce attacks by the Serbian army, but has since been restored and reopened after the war. Already in the late 1990s Dubrovnik regained its international reputation as one of the most popular tourist destinations.

Dubrovnik minted its own money for a long time, from the late 13th to the 19th century, producing nearly 20 different currencies, including minca, solad, dinar, ariluk, perpera, skuda, talir, and libertine. In 1723 Dubrovnik began making silver currency. On the front side was the image of the patron St. Blaise and on the reverse the stem of Dubrovnik City.

Freedom ("Libertas") has always been regarded as the greatest value of Dubrovnik. The flag of Dubrovnik, adopted in 1418 with the abolition of slave trading, has always had the inscription "Libertas." Indeed the Republic of Dubrovnik was one of the first to abolish slavery. The inscription, in Latin, above the entrance to Fort Lovrijenac reads: ***non bene prototo libertas venditur auro***. "Liberty cannot be given away for all the gold in the world." Dubrovnik has lived under this motto for centuries. At the opening of the Summer Festival, the immortal verses of the famous Croatian writer, Ivan Gundulic, are performed: "O you beautiful, o you dear, o you precious freedom…all the silver, all the gold, all human lives cannot be a pay for your pure beauty…"

As you visit the City the first thing that captures your attention is the Stradun, Dubrovnik's main street and the center of the City's pulsating life, a popular meeting place for local inhabitants and tourists alike. You will probably find it surprising that the Stradun used to be a sea channel dividing the Slavic settlement at the foot of Srd Mountain and Laus Island in the southern part of the city. In the 12th century the town was united by filling in the channel. Later on it was paved and nowadays it is one of the key symbols of Dubrovnik, home to more than 40,000 inhabitants. Stradun is also architecturally unique in that nearly all the ground floors of the adjoinin g buildings used for trade have entry doors constructed on an angle, combining the door and a window spanned by a semicircular arch. The door is kept closed and goods are handed over the windows sill, which serves as a counter. The citizens of Dubrovnik are justifiably proud of their aqueduct and Onofrio's Fountains, named after Onofrio de Giordano de la Cava who was hired from Naples in the 15th century to complete many hydraulic engineering works for the city. The fountains are a part of the water supply channel system that was created to bring water from a well in Rijeka Dubrovacka located 20 kilometers from the fountains to the Stradun The epigraph on the fountains witnesses the difficulty of this hydraulic construction that was considered to be a masterpiece of that time. The aqueduct and both the big and small fountains were crucial for hygienic conditions of the city as well as for the development of the textile industry.

Dubrovnik has had public health care since the 14th century. It was the first port to introduce quarantine for passengers and ships, unlike Venice that would block the trade by forbidding entrance to the port, Dubrovnik only delayed it in the case of justified suspicion of infectious disease. Quarantines lasted 40 days, after which a sanitary official named ***kacamorat*** would decide whether the quarantined person, held on an island outside Dubrovnik, could enter the city. The quarantine system lasted during the entire period of the free independent republic, four and a half centuries.

In the 15th century the city founded its first orphanage to shelter abandoned children and reduce the incidence of infanticide. Before the foundation of the orphanage, women would leave their unwanted children at church entrances, doors of good neighbors, or simply on the street. The penalty for proven infanticide was death by hanging; however, there is no evidence that such an execution ever took place. The men were not held to moral or legal obligation for extramarital children. The children in the orphanage were mostly the fruit of forbidden relationships between aristocrats and their servants, or marital infidelities. Orphaned children were released at age six to adopting families as a potential labor source.

Regulation of sexual behavior by the Republic was strict. A rapist had to pay a fine or lose both eyes and would escape punishment only if he agreed to marry the victim with her consent. The traditional penalty for homosexual or pedophiliac sodomy was decapitation. Persecution of homosexuals continued into the 1980s until the expansion of tourism opened the door to homosexuality and eventually even the organization of world homosexual congresses in Dubrovnik.

Similarly, marriage followed strict conditions, including a premarital contract for engagement and commitment. The grounds for contracting a marriage were family name, origin, belongings and stability. The future bride would bring a dowry in gold and real estate whereas the future groom would have to guarantee the equivalent value with his belongings. The marriage was arranged by parents or relatives during the very early age of the future bride (between the age of 8 and 12) and could be contracted when she became sexually mature, but not before the age of 16. Bigamy was a crime therefore, children from secret marriages held no legal right to their father's property.

Criminal punishment in the Republic of Dubrovnik followed specific public rituals that were developed and modified throughout the centuries. The porch of Rector's Palace functioned as the official courthouse. Before passing sentence, the court would have the accused kneel down, confess his guilt, and thank the judges for their justness. Sentences to death were by public hanging at Dance (park Gradac which is still known by the name "Gallows"). For minor crimes, sinners would be tied to the column of shame and exposed to all possible insults such as spitting and hitting. Thieves and violators of public order were made to march down the square and Stradun holding a donkey's tail and wearing a shameful hat and were marked by recognizable details of their crime such a bag of garbage around the neck of a polluter. Some violators were exiled to the island of St. Andrews others were walled in small cells at the portside where they were soaked with sea water and would often died.

At the south part of City Walls stands Fortress of St. Ivan, a master work of Paskoje Milicevic, a citizen of Dubrovnik. It was quite important as it was used to prevent the harbor from pirates and other enemies. During the night, citizens of Dubrovnik would close the port entry by stretching heavy chains under the water, from the fortress to the breakwater preventing ships from entering the city. Nowadays the ground floor hosts the Aquarium and on the upper floor, the Ethnographic and Maritime Museum.

Dubrovnik life is not all rules and regulations, however. Dubrovnikians are as fun loving people as in other mediterranean countries. The Lindo is the most popular dance in the city. Its performance is a true synergy of musical and almost theatrical experience. The key instrument is called "***lijerica***" which was an old South Dalmatian instrument with three strings, originally coming from the eastern Mediterranean. The dance master plays sitting down with his lijerica on his left knee and stomping with his right foot in order to dictate the rhythm to the dancers. The dancers move in a circle around the dance master, whose commands in rhyme are quite humorous and ambiguous. He also decides who will dance with whom and announces changes of dance figures, encouraging the dancers to compete in entertainig improvisations. The origin of the name "Lindo" is of a recent date - some say that it was named after legendary dance master Nikola Lale Lindo, whereas others believe that it refers to the local name for "lijerica" player. The Summer Festival, one of the greatest Croatian cultural manifestations, takes place in the period between July 10th and August 25th. Hot summer evenings host performances and concerts that take place in the unique scenery of old architecture and cultural heritage, transforming the entire city into a stage. The festival starts with a proclamation from Orlando's Column in Luza Square followed by 45 days of celebration, featuring various artists and revivals of traditional

Renaissance theatre. During the opening ceremony Sponza Palace has a unique role. The protagonist of this ceremony impersonates the Rector who, with members of the Council, greets the actors that come to entertain the public with their plays and music.. Different venues such as squares, churches, forts, city streets and public gardens welcome the performers from the national and international music and theatre circuit. Some of the most famous national authors whose works are performed are Marin Drzic, Ivan Gundulic, Ivo Vojnovic, along with traditional performances of Shakespeare, Carlo Goldoni, Moliere, and Greek tragedians.

At Orlando's Column you can truly sense the rhythm of everyday city life. This stone column proudly presents a statue of Roland, the legendary knight of Charlemagne, symbolizing the people's wish for the freedom of the Republic of Dubrovnik. In the past, all decrees and notices of the Republic were proclaimed from the statue. The column also had commercial uses. The forearm of the statue was used in the Middle Ages as a unit of measurement for fabric, one of the first recorded units of length in Europe.

Dubrovnik is home to many notable poets, playwrights, painters, mathematicians, physicists and, accordingly, one of the main centers for the development of the Croatian language and literature. Marin Drzic, the writer and chronicler of the Dubrovnik Republic, is undoubtedly one of the biggest authors of comedies in Renaissance literature, a true predecessor of the famous Moliere. The works of Ivan Gundulic and other Dubrovnik authors have similarly influenced the way Dubrovnikians speak and write in Croatian.

One of the curiosities that inevitably attract your attention in Dubrovnik is a Renaissance owl facemask on the Franciscan monastery. It used to be a drainage spout; nowadays, the rain no longer flows through its mouth. There is a special ritual that is still preserved and practiced by citizens of Dubrovnik and even more by its visitors. You need to climb the very slippery owl facemask, finding wall holes, take off your shirt, turn around and put it on again. According to legend, if you succeed, you will find true love. Whether for luck in love or not, citizens and visitors still attempt to climb the mask, mostly during nighttime as failure is considered to be a shame. Yet the owl will keep your secret, so… do dare!

The cult of Saint Blaise, patron and protector of Dubrovnik, dates back to the 10th century when Venetians plotted to take over the city. According to legend, Saint Blaise spoke to citizen Stojka at night while he was praying in the church to inform the city of Venetian intentions. As a result the city was successfully defended and the citizens in gratitude proclaimed Saint Blaise to be their patron. His image became the city's symbol of sovereignty and was depicted on almost all paintings, reliefs and flags. The celebration of St. Blaise takes place every year on the 3rd day of February, a lively preservation of Dubrovnik's folklore heritage. During this festivity the Saint's relics are carried out in the procession along with various plays and folk performances that unite the citizens in celebration of their freedom. The most precious sculpture of Dubrovnik is the golden statue of the patron holding a model of the city, which on that day is placed on the main altar in Saint Blaise's Church. Moreover, the statue is considered to be miraculous as it was undamaged in the earthquake and fire of 1667. Pile Gate is the western entrance to the Old Town; due to its strategic importance Fort Lovrijenac was built on the rocks just beneath. It is the only fort that was not an integral part of the City Walls. There is a stone bridge within its two Gothic arches ending at another wooden bridge. That wooden drawbridge used to be pulled up every evening; nowadays, the statue of city patron St. Blaise over the arch dominates the entrance.

Maritime tradition has always had a significant role for the citizens of Dubrovnik and some of the older customs are still preserved. When passing the channel between the island of Lokrum and the City the seamen always salute their hometown by sounding the ships' sirens. The City's inhabitants, especially the women, respond by waving bed sheets from their windows. In addition, whenever they pass the Lady of Danaca church in the small cove next to the northwestern part of the City walls, the seamen sound the ships' sirens in salute and the nuns in return give them their blessing by ringing the church bells. Dating to the 15th century the Lady of Danaca church is a favorite sanctuary of Dubrovnik's citizens, especially seamen.

A true adventure in Dubrovnik is not complete unless you take a walk along the extensive labyrinthine City Walls. These intriguing corridors create a discovery of a different perspective of the urban centre that appears as an open pearl shell. The walls were built from the 13th to the 17th century. This impressive system of turrets and towers secured major points with fortifications intended to protect the city from attacks. The City Walls are one of the symbols of its freedom and one of the largest and best preserved fortification systems in Europe.

Prologue

As I walked through the walls of the ancient city, Dubrovnik provoked inside me many sensations. With the passage of time, I attempted to capture those feelings in this book, which is at once a proposition, a search as well as a photographic essay.

The city with its textures and history can set the visitor's pace as it did for me. It is a walled town with neither army nor king; always a place of curiosity, beauty, mystery and desire. Dubrovnik was a point of balance between the West and the East a gateway to a place of magic, which provocatively transports the visitor through time.

Walking the Stradum, stepping on every Stria stone, one daydreams, feeling that this sense of mystery and magic has always been there, throughout time. Mentioning the Stria stone is not a mere detail; the stone is the raw material that was so often sought by empires to build their most beautiful and precious monuments. Its magnificence is felt in its silky texture, glossy polish and its color of liquid sand, somewhere between a beige and cream that changes magically with the light of day.

All of this frames the dreamlike quality which I wanted to give this book. A succession of images marked by a rhythm of cadenza and pauses, trying to show the purest essence of the place, rather than a precise guide. I hope these Photographs recreate these sensations and feelings to be preserved in our memory along with the city itself.

Fernando Espinosa Chauvin

DUBROVAČKI PISAC
HRVATSKI SHAKESPEARE, GOETHE, DANTE, MOLIERE
MARIN DRŽIĆ

Skiny
IVO GRBIĆ
·DUM MARINU U ČAST·
Vidra
1508. 500. 2008.
OBLJETNICA ROĐENJA

SANITAT
DUBROVNIK

DB 3156
DB787

1834.

FERNANDO ESPINOSA CHAUVIN

New York based photographer whose latest works include ***Afrodisiaco*** (a gourmet food book blending beautiful models with fabulous food creations in a dramatic setting); ***Trococo*** (an innovative approach to the colorful world of drag queens blending Rococo art with their creative costumes and displaying an unprejudicial view of their beauty, style and grace); and ***The Gates*** (a photographic essay of Christo's installation in 2005 recreating the mood and feeling of that extraordinary artwork in Central Park New York in winter).

He is currently working on several other projects including ***The Chocolate Journey (the story of Ecuadorian chocolate from Cacao Plantation to European delicacy)*** and ***The Galapagos*** (a photographic journey in black and white of this unique and exciting place).

He got his first camera at the age of 12 and developed his interest in Photography at his school newspaper in Ecuador. He received his first National Prize at age 17 for his photographs of ***Scenes of Quito***. He later had an exhibit at the Casa de Cultura in Ecuador and went on to win other institutional prizes.

His professional photography career began in New York as a fashion photographer for international modeling agencies such as Ford Models, Elite, IMG, and Next and later expanded into architectural assignments for magazines and brochures, carrying over his eye for lighting and design to those compositions. He has taught illumination techniques in photography at workshops hosted by the International Center of Photography in New York and by the gallery "Conteiner-Pobre Diablo" in Quito. His professional work has been shown in art galleries, and published in various magazines and catalogues, in both the United States and Ecuador.